Why People Leave…And What You Can Do About It

A Guide to Leadership Awesomeness

To my beautiful wife – In all ways, always

To my exceptional children – Do what you love doing, do it with passion, do it with integrity and do it as much as you possibly can.

Why People Leave...And What You Can Do About It

A Guide to Leadership Awesomeness

Ryan C. Haskell

Publisher:
WritingCaddie.com
9948 Heather Ridge Trail
Frisco, TX 75034
505-269-6999

This publication is intended to provide accurate and authoritative information with regard to the subject matter covered. It is offered with the understanding that neither the publisher nor the author is engaged in rendering legal, tax or other professional advice or services. If legal, tax or other expert assistance is needed, the services of a competent professional should be sought.

This book is intended for instructional purposes only. Readers are advised to proceed with the techniques described herein with caution. Neither the author nor publisher makes any warranties, expressed or implied, about the merchantability or fitness for any particular use of this product.

C O N T E N T S

INTRODUCTION

PART I: WHY PEOPLE LEAVE

PART II: WHAT YOU CAN DO ABOUT IT

- ➢ Create the Vision and Turn it into Reality
- ➢ Use Simple Math to Build Your Team
- ➢ Get the Right People on the Bus and In the Right Seats

- ➢ Cast Your Leadership Shadow
- ➢ Give Yourself Permission to Steal
- ➢ The Speed of the Leader Determines the Rate of the Pack

- ➢ Establish a Winning Culture
- ➢ Focus on Results, Not Effort
- ➢ Don't Accept Mediocrity or Below

Introduction

As I considered the title and foundation of this book I tried to put myself in the mindset of a young professional, not an author. Yes, there has to be linguistic integrity, but I am not writing this as a professional author that has spent years and years conducting betas, interviewing focus groups and dynamic business leaders, and researching the findings of "experts" in the field of leadership. This book, or better yet this guide, is a common sense approach to leadership based on several years of observing, admiring, questioning, admonishing, and despising leadership styles of my superiors, peers, and subordinates.

The great coaches, military brass, and business leaders of the past and present often write books detailing their leadership styles and successes. I have read many of these books and I have enjoyed several different perspectives, stories, and anecdotes.

The primary thing that separates this guide from other books, other than most who wrote these other books have much more fame and fortune than I do, is that I have never been a coach of a championship team, never served in the military, nor have ever been a CEO. Most of my career has been spent in mid-level management. I have a great wife and two kids, drive modest cars and live in a modest home. I have changed companies a few times over the years and spend my free time at my kids' practices and events, watching TV, surfing the Web, and hanging out with friends. In other words, I am just like the vast majority of people who will read this book. That is what separates this guide, I think for the better, from other literature on leadership.

Before going any further, it is important to define and discuss leadership and its characteristics. Merriam-Webster defines a *leader* as "a person who has commanding authority or influence." There are two things that, in my opinion, go well beyond a simple definition regarding a *leader* or *leadership*. First and foremost, a leader must have a proven and verifiable history of producing positive results. Make no mistake, every facet of life seeks those who produce results. However, producing results alone does not guarantee you entry into the exclusive "leader" club. Second, a title does not guarantee, or even suggest, earning leader status. These two things are mutually exclusive. Results alone, a management title alone, or results and a management title together do not guarantee leader status.

So now that we have confused things thoroughly, we must ask the question then of what earns a person the distinction of being called a leader. Sorry to disappoint you, but ultimately I think this question is extremely difficult, if not impossible, to answer. There are so many variables, so many styles, so many perceptions, and most of all every person in our world is a unique individual and defines leadership differently. My definition is embedded later in the guide.

For now, we will focus not on my definition of leadership, but rather two more critical questions that provide more relevance to the credibility of this guide. First, what makes me qualified to write a guide on leadership? Second, if leadership has a variable definition, then how can you be assured that the examples and anecdotes in this guide are right?

The answer to the first question is simple. I have observed and I have learned. I have questioned and I have learned. I have succeeded and I have learned. I have failed and I have learned. I am simply putting on to paper what I have *learned* that I strongly believe, if used effectively, will prepare an individual to lead today's workforce.

The answer to the second question is a little trickier. It's not about being right. It's about sharing leadership approaches that I have seen be successful time and time again either by another or myself. Then it is your job to decipher what is right for you. Admittedly, I strongly believe that the more of these leadership approaches that you adopt and execute will lead you to greater success levels.

I will include names to provide credit where credit is due, but I prefer to focus on approaches, common sense approaches that is, that leaders whom I believe are extremely effective *and* produce positive results display. That, in a nutshell, is the premise of the guide.

The last thing about the guide you need to know before we jump in is that each chapter, or rather each approach, are not written to normal, lengthy standards. This is a guide and therefore should provide examples and anecdotes. However, part of being an effective leader, or in this case learning to become a more effective leader, is knowing when to use fifty words instead of one hundred. Also, be keenly aware that effective leaders prefer, and often demand, to-the-point, bottom-line verbiage in oral or written communications. To that end, let's jump in.

RCH

Part I

Why People Leave

CHAPTER 1

Why People Leave

"If you cannot work with love but only with distaste, it is better that you should leave your work." --- *Kahlil Gibran*

WHY PEOPLE LEAVE

The foundation of this guide is to provide you tried and true leadership tactics and methods that will help you become a more effective leader. However, truly effective leaders not only understand how to effectively lead individuals and teams to execute on plans and deliver results, they understand the individuality of people. Specifically what makes them want to stay and grow or what makes them want to leave. Many studies and polling have been done rating employee satisfaction within the American workforce. On average, 50 percent of Americans are dissatisfied with their job, which obviously means that, on average, only 50 are satisfied (but only 14 percent are very satisfied!). Additional polling shows 40 percent are dissatisfied with their work-life balance and that number jumps to 70 percent for managers.[1]

So why do people leave? The answer to this has so many variables and is ultimately an individual decision. However, many articles and books have been written detailing the primary reasons dissatisfied workers leave their jobs and/or companies. Some of the more prominent include, but are not limited to:

- Unmet expectations
- Few rewards for good behavior
- A mismatch of skills
- Resentment of being micromanaged
- Lack of coaching and feedback
- Underutilized or unchallenged
- Limited growth opportunities
- Faced with unreasonable demands

- Overworked
- Not apprised of changes in the organization
- Loss of confidence in senior leaders

Whatever the reason or multitude of reasons, quality leaders not only recognize these but try to mitigate the negative impact of them with effective communication and respecting the individuality of people.

In my opinion, an effective leader must first understand why people leave before they can truly lead people to stay and have a positive impact on the group and/or organization. Unfortunately, too many times we try to force our leadership style on our team members, which is okay to a point, instead of adapting our leadership strengths to the individuality of the person or group. Then, as is so often the case, the person leaves and we never find out why our talented people leave.

Part II

What You Can Do About It

CHAPTER 2

Planning and Organization

> ➢ **CREATE THE VISION AND TURN IT INTO REALITY**

> ➢ **USE SIMPLE TO MATH TO BUILD YOUR TEAM**

> ➢ **GET THE RIGHT PEOPLE ON THE BUS AND IN THE RIGHT SEATS**

"He who fails to plan, plans to fail" --- *Proverb*

CREATE THE VISION AND TURN IT INTO REALITY

There are many different definitions of vision not only in dictionaries, but amongst business leaders as well. One of the simplest and best I have heard is that it is the "owner's vision of what the business is – and should and could be."[2] The word owner can be replaced with board of directors, CEO, or any other leadership role. For the sake of this text, we will adopt this definition. If you want to become a true leader, you will instinctively "own" your portion of the business so the word owner is universally applicable.

One of the biggest mistakes I see young managers make is that they don't create a vision for their business. When I say business, I don't necessarily mean a business one personally owns, although that definitely applies too, but rather business in terms of the part of the organization one is designated to lead.

Most companies, especially large ones, have a vision established by the board of directors, the CEO, the executive leadership team, or a combination of the aforementioned. Many young managers adopt this vision as their own. While it is important to understand and frequently share the vision of the company, often that vision applies to the global entity and will not necessarily help you lead your business unit. For example, a company that previously employed me had a vision to be the most preferred sales distribution partner for wireless, broadband and media carriers across the US. This is a great vision but had little to do with day-to-day leadership of my region, or business. Yes, the productivity that came out of my business could and should contribute to the company's vision, but I needed a vision for my business. My vision was essentially to be the benchmark in which other business units within the organization would be measured and to be the feeding ground for the future leaders in our organization.

There are numerous resources on the Internet to help a leader create a vision for their business. Remember, however, that a vision is different than a mission. A vision is what you want your business to become, a foreshadowing of sorts. A mission is the purpose or reason for the business's existence. My mission statement, for example, was to deliver sales and financial results above the company's expectations, provide measurably first-class customer service, maintain a widely accepted reputation of being a valued community asset and, most importantly, supply significant personal and professional growth opportunities to our team members.

Your first step toward great leadership is upon you. It's now time for you to create the vision for your business.

Vision:

_____

_____

_____

_____

_____

_____

_____

_____

_____

Don't cheat yourself by moving past the blank lines. You must create your vision before moving forward. Great. You have now completed your vision. Or at least you think you have. Unfortunately, that is the easy part. The more difficult task is to turn that vision into reality. You can have the best vision, mission or business plan known to man. You can prepare contingency and exit strategies. All of these are key elements in effective leadership, but the main theme here is that they are all written on paper.

Scott Isaacs, my great friend mentioned throughout the guide, frequently talks about this with prospective and current leaders of his organization. He simply asks, "What are you doing to turn your vision into reality? Arguably the worst answer is "I don't have a vision." As a leader you may not immediately realize what just happened, but without being physical struck you just got slapped right across the face. Why? A leader should have previously known they did not have one and assisted in developing one.

Assuming that you have a vision when the question of turning it into reality is asked, I am strongly encouraging you to not answer "I am not sure" or "I don't know." Let me be clear. It is not a vision if you have no intent to turn it into reality. Paper leaders are as ineffective as micromanagers (discussed later in the guide). You can have the best plans on paper, but they mean nothing until they are executed upon.

I referenced earlier in this section that you had completed your vision, or at least you thought you had. I encourage you to review the previous page where you wrote your vision and truly answer yourself as to whether you have the intent to turn your vision into reality and if it is conceivable that it can be turned into reality. If the answer is yes, congratulations, you have now completed your vision for your business. If the answer is no, then I encourage you re-write your vision below that you intend to turn into reality and that is conceivable of turning into reality.

New Vision:

_____

_____

_____

_____

_____

_____

_____

_____

Congratulations. Now it's time, right now, to start turning your vision into reality. Turning vision into reality may potentially be a long and laborious process. On the other hand, it may be short and relatively painless. Turning vision into reality means different things to different leaders. In fact, this topic alone may be the foundation for a completely different book. I do know, however, that sitting around will never turn your vision to turn into reality. Thomas Edison, the great American inventor, once said "Opportunity is missed by most people because it is dressed in overalls and looks like work." Turning your vision into reality in today's world requires you to, at minimum, execute on the fine points of this guide.

USE SIMPLE MATH TO BUILD YOUR TEAM

For all the extravagant data and analysis that exists in corporate America today, increasing team talent is as easy as using simple addition, subtraction, and division. You're probably thinking it can't be that easy. And you're right, kind of. It's never easy to find great people. But what is easy is using simple math to increase team talent. Let me explain.

Assume you have 10 direct reports. We attach a simple grading scale for your team members based on your organization's expectations of performance. In this example we will use five as exemplary, four is above average or strong performer, three is average or developing, two is below average or needs improvement, and one is, well, poor. Of your 10, one is exemplary, four are strong performers, two are average or developing, two are below average or need improvement, and one is poor (I will assume you didn't hire this person). Multiply the number of team members in each category by the corresponding grade. Add up the total grade of all 10 of your direct reports. In this example, the total is 32. Now divide 32 by your 10 total team members to get the average grade of your team. Simple division tells us that the team talent average is 3.2. This score is obviously indicates a team grade slightly above average.

At minimum, it is unacceptable to have an average performer on your team (unless they are still developing) let alone a below average or poor performer. So let's focus on the poor performer. If you haven't already, it's immediately time to coach them up or coach them out. Remember, don't accept mediocrity or below or you will find yourself getting coached up or coached out. Upon termination of your poor performer, you now have an open position on your team. When backfilling a position, it is never acceptable to maintain or degridate the team talent.

In short and barring any unforeseen or extraordinary circumstances, you should never hire below your team talent score. Logically speaking then, you know that you must hire or promote someone whose talent is higher than 3.2. Simply put, you must hire a four or a five. If you hire a four, your average team talent score goes from 3.2 to 3.5, a strong number. If you hire a five, it goes from 3.2 to 3.6. Please don't construe that because the impact to the overall average only increases slightly with the hiring of a five instead of a four, that you should seek fours instead of fives. The bottom line is that generally only 10 – 20 percent of an existing team is exemplary over the long-term. New teams may have no exemplary members. Therefore you must be realistic about your hiring expectations.

Now that you have graded your team and decided to make changes, it is now time to get the right people on the bus and in the right seats.

GET THE RIGHT PEOPLE ON THE BUS AND IN THE RIGHT SEATS

Getting the right people on the bus is symbolic of simply getting the right people on your team and/or in your organization. Getting them in the right seats is representative of making sure they have the correct role within the team or organization. Of all the concepts detailed in this guide, these may be the most difficult to execute. By no means, however, is it impossible and your effort and diligence in this cause is critical to your leadership success. Technically, they are two different concepts, but they are so closely related that they are often discussed simultaneously. I prefer to discuss them sequentially.

Getting the right people on the bus requires patience and discipline. There are many barriers that get in the way of bringing on the right people. The compensation you can offer, the desire and timeframe of the potential candidate, the availability of an opening on your team, the HR department, and the benefits of your company, just to name a few. As in other parts of life and leadership, seek to understand, but do not focus on the barriers.

If you are convinced that a person must be on your team, usually because of a personal experience or personal recommendation from a trusted source, then your focus should be on courting that person similarly to the way you would court a life partner. Remember, the continuous improvement and evolution of a team is critical to your long term success. There are certain people that you realize must be on your team regardless of whether they are available or not or whether there is even a position available on your team at the time.

In the past I had an interview with a large wireless service provider prior to a position with them even being available. Changes in the company were imminent and their goal was to simply indentify quality candidates that they wanted on the team without knowing their specific seat on the bus at the time. This is the essence of the getting the right people on the bus. Jim Calhoun, the legendary men's basketball coach from the University of Connecticut, once stated that over the years he had learned a lot about leadership but his biggest realization was that effective leadership was more about the Jimmy's and the Joe's and not the X's and the O's.

Once you have courted the right the people, it is now time to get them in the right seats on the bus. The right people will always do a good job. The right people in the right seats will almost always excel. So how does an effective leader know when a person is in the right seat? You will know by the productivity, the feedback from those that work either directly or indirectly with that person, and by the attitude and body language displayed by that person. Just as with an uncomfortable article of clothing, you can generally feel when someone is not comfortable.

During one of my stops along the way as a sales manager, I inherited an account manager, Mike Kelly, who was relatively new to his position. Over time he developed into a solid account manager, but there always seemed to be something missing even by his own admission. He was very strong in product knowledge, training, organization, time management, work ethic, and was well-liked across the board. However, Mike was less adept at business development and having straight-forward, difficult conversations with people, which were critical components of the position. It's not to say Mike was not willing to accept these tasks, but rather there was always a general discomfort in performing them. That discomfort, even with all his strengths in other areas, never allowed him to go from good to great in his account manager role. Mike was the right person and a person I always knew needed to be on the team somewhere. He was just in the wrong seat at Alltel.

In my next my endeavor, I assisted in the recruitment of Mike into a training and talent recruitment role. Training and recruiting generally requires product knowledge, organization, time management, work ethic and being well-liked and respected. These were Mike's strengths and he excelled in every facet of his training and recruiting role immediately upon arrival. His impact was felt throughout the organization. This is the essence of not only getting the right people on the bus, but also getting them in right seats.

These two critical components of effective leadership are not mutually exclusive. As mentioned earlier in the chapter, these two are often discussed simultaneously, which is appropriate, but can and should be accepted sequentially as well. After all, the right seat is not always going to be immediately open for the right person. The ultimate goal is to get the right people on the bus and in the right seats, but the first goal is to get to the right people on the bus.

CHAPTER 3

Identify and Develop Leaders

- ➢ **CAST YOUR LEADERSHIP SHADOW**

- ➢ **GIVE YOURSELF PERMISSION TO STEAL**

- ➢ **THE SPEED OF THE LEADER DETERMINES THE RATE OF THE PACK**

"The function of leadership is to produce more leaders, not more followers." --- Ralph Nader

CAST YOUR LEADERSHIP SHADOW

An effective leader is not only responsible for leading the group for which they have been charged or have chosen to lead, but also to develop other leaders within that group. Developing other leaders is not only important to that group, but will assuredly benefit the individuals and organization down the road. Part of a leader's responsibility is to leave the group and/or organization in better shape than they found it, and part of doing that is developing a leader or leaders to take on the role should the current leader move on. This is the meaning of casting your leadership shadow.

I mentioned at the beginning of the guide that I would prefer focusing on leadership approaches as opposed to names. However, I did say that I would throw out names to drive home a point. Tom Landry, the legendary former head coach of the Dallas Cowboys, and Bill Walsh, the former head coach of the San Francisco 49ers, both of the National Football League, are exemplary examples of casting your leadership shadow. Not only did they produce positive results, a requirement of an effective leader, they developed other leaders simultaneously while producing those positive results.

Tom Landry, who brought the Cowboys to five Superbowls, winning two of them, hired and developed five assistant coaches that eventually became head coaches in the NFL. Mike Ditka won a Superbowl leading the Chicago bears and Dan Reeves took four teams to Superbowls. The other coaches were Gene Stallings, Dick Nolan, and John Mackovic.

Bill Walsh, the head coach of the 49ers from 1979 to 1988, arguably casted his leadership shadow better than any coach in NFL history. Not only did the 49ers win three Superbowls during his 10-year tenure, seven assistant coaches during his tenure went on to become head coaches in the NFL. George Seifert went on to coach two Superbowl winning teams with the 49ers and Mike Holmgren went on to win one with the Green Bay Packers. In fact, 11 of the 29 head coaches (38%) in the 25 Superbowls following his hiring in 1979 were disciples of Bill Walsh.[3] The other five coaches were Sam Wyche, Dennis Green, Mike White, Jim Fassel, and Ray Rhodes. As if this wasn't impressive enough, several assistant coaches under these seven have also went on to become head coaches in the NFL. Bill Walsh casted an enormous leadership shadow.

The success of Landry and Walsh and others like them are not accidental. There are three critical components in developing leaders. First, you must identify potential leaders. Second, you must allow them to make mistakes and coach to those mistakes. Finally, you must include them in your leadership role, and not just the fun or glorious stuff.

GIVE YOURSELF PERMISSION TO STEAL

Steal within the boundaries of the law and ethical behavior, that is. Despite popular opinion, great leaders are not born they are made. What's more is that they are generally made as a result of lessons, both conscious and subconscious, they experience throughout their life. The lessons are also positive and negative. Think of the times, whether playing sports as a youth or as an entry level employee, that you've said 'when I get to lead a group, I want to lead just like her.' Conversely, and probably more often, think of the times you have said "wow, when I get to lead a team I am going to do the exact opposite of everything he does." These are feelings we have all had. The leadership style you use today, or will use in the future, is a result of these feelings. In short, you stole them. That's okay. For the purposes of becoming an effective leader, I am giving you permission to steal. Steal shamelessly and often.

To this day, if there is something I hear or see that is thought provoking or insightful that will help me become a better leader and person, I either write it down immediately or send myself a text or email so I will remember it. Many of the chapters in this book came from regular conversations with family, friends, and colleagues that I thought were relatively insignificant at the time. Yes, I am a great thief.

If you think I came up with all of this great stuff in the book by myself, I appreciate the confidence and trust you *had* in me. My wife, Kristal, my mom and dad, Connie and Dave, my brothers, Erick and Craig, my father in-law, Jerry, Warren Bradshaw, Bill Fowler, George Haskell (my Bumpa), Steve Parker, Jon Freier, James Kirby, Amy

McCune, Kim Algya, Wayne Taack, Monty Hoppel, Forrest Allen, Coach Strobel, Coach Skarwecki, Coach Clabaugh, Coach Ramharter, Shannon Susman, Richard Graves, Dina Pettlon, Phyllis Marshall, Todd Heiner, Darren Yager, Jeff Heuple, Mario Otero, Bill Wallace, Scott Isaacs, Tom Connette, to name a few, have been instrumental in the development of my leadership traits. Most were instrumental in helping me learn what I should do and some were instrumental in helping me learn what I should not do. In most cases, they didn't even know I stole from them. So for that I am eternally grateful.

I wrote this list of people for two reasons. One, I wanted to acknowledge the people that have helped me along the way. Two, and more importantly, I wanted to cast my leadership shadow and encourage you to write out a list of people that have helped you along the way and what specifically they contributed (meaning what did you steal from them?). Understand that 'helped' doesn't necessarily equal a positive experience. Just as we tend to learn more from our mistakes, we tend to learn more from our negative experiences. Give those people credit too. This will allow you take your experiences and develop a leadership style or contribute to your existing one.

THE SPEED OF THE LEADER DETERMINES THE RATE OF THE PACK

This is a simple, self-explanatory concept, yet critical to effective leadership. I immediately think of the world-famous Iditarod race held in Alaska each year when considering this concept. The Iditarod race allows up to 16 Alaskan Huskies per Musher (driver) to participate in the race, all of which are lined up in pairs behind the single leader.[4] The lead dog's responsibility is to set the pace for the rest of the dogs and lead the turns when necessary. Hence the phraseology, the speed of the leader determines the rate of the pack.

The key word in this leadership trait is *speed*. Speed, as it relates to this concept, can be defined in several different ways. The list includes, but is not limited to, work ethic, initiative, knowledge, ability, experience, integrity, respect earned, passion, determination, intuition, or a combination of the aforementioned. What is important to understand is that while several people on a given team or in a given group may possess these characteristics, it is the leaders' speed, or at least the perception of the leaders' speed, that sets the pace of the team either positively or negatively.

Notice that some of the characteristics are learned and/or earned and some may be inherent. It is extremely difficult, if not impossible, to lead only with learned or earned characteristics or conversely with only inherent traits. It has often been stated that someone "was just born to lead" and while I believe there is a lot of truth to that, remember that a requirement of a leader is to have a proven and verifiable record of producing positive results. So, yes, one needs those inherent traits, but also must have the learned and/or earned characteristics.

There are two primary lessons here. First, it is important to make sure not to self-proclaim oneself or another a leader simply based on learned and/or earned characteristics alone or inherent traits alone. The only effective leaders with whom I have come in contact are those that possess a combination of learned and/or earned characteristics *and* inherent traits.

Second, it is essential to understand that these learned and/or earned characteristics and inherent traits work both ways. We have primarily discussed these in a positive realm. However, if work ethic, initiative, knowledge, ability, experience, integrity, respect earned, passion, determination, intuition, or a combination of the aforementioned are lackluster, then the speed of the leader will be poor and thus the rate of the pack will likely be poor.

Your critical mission as a leader is to set a speedy, but efficient and effective, pace for your team to follow. If the lead dog goes too fast, the team behind them gets tired and unproductive. If the lead dog goes too slowly, the team doesn't reach its full potential. Either way, the team loses. Set a speed that promotes winning for your team and the organization.

CHAPTER 4

Drive Toward and Achieve Results

- ➢ **ESTABLISH A WINNING CULTURE**

- ➢ **FOCUS ON RESULTS, NOT EFFORT**

- ➢ **DON'T ACCEPT MEDIOCRITY OR BELOW**

"A business like an automobile, has to be driven, in order to get results"
--- B.C. Forbes

ESTABLISH A WINNING CULTURE

There is no better feeling in leadership than when your team is more concerned with letting you down or the other members of the team more than they are concerned with their own personal accolades and accomplishments. This is my definition of a winning culture. This, of course, is something you as a leader would never admit to out loud, especially to your team. It is also not a burden you want your team to carry. But secretly, you have reached the apex of leadership when this happens and you now know that you have a winning culture within your team. This is no easy task to accomplish and it can take months or even years to accomplish.

As with most successful things, it starts with people. You have to recruit, hire, train, coach, and develop people that are willing to share success and failure with others, have a commitment to integrity and strong work ethic, have been winners in past environments, and that have the ability to promote the vision for the greater good even in the absence of leadership. This is not an all-inclusive list and these people are not easy to find (refer to the section on getting the right people on the bus and in the right seats).

While I have hired and worked with my share of dogs in the past, I have been part of two such teams that encapsulated the spirit of a winning culture. One of which I was lucky enough to be the leader. Cody Cornoyer, Billy Kimbler, Mike Kelly, Christie Armijo, Bobby Hollis, Julio Samble, and Bill Wallace were the heroes of establishing our winning culture. We had young and old, male and female, three different ethnic backgrounds, and yet were capable of accomplishing extraordinary things often as a result of peer coaching. This was truly a special team that was assembled under my leadership.

Establishing standards and expectations and providing them in writing is also a key component to a winning culture. How many times in your career have you started a new position and understood what your job responsibilities were, but did not have a grasp on the standards and expectations of working within the team or organization? Unfortunately, it happens more often than not. Establishing a winning culture is reliant upon everyone knowing and understanding the standards and expectations of themselves as well as others. For example, during each one of my weekly team meetings with the aforementioned team, I rotated team members and had one take a portion of the meeting and discuss a topic that would benefit all of us. It could range from sales tactics to success stories to product or services training to leadership. This was a standard and expectation and everyone knew it. Initially, there was some hesitation. Eventually, it became a desired portion of our meetings and part of the winning culture we established.

A third component of establishing a winning culture is constant and consistent communication and reinforcement. Our team meetings were an example of this. Establishing a winning culture is an all the time thing. As the leader, you should praise the actions and results consistent with the standards and expectations. Conversely, if a person or group of people on your team are acting or performing in a manner inconsistent with the standards and expectations of your winning culture, they must immediately be introduced to the *Tion* brothers (see page 44). Like cancer in the human body, a cancer within your team can spread and cause severe damage or destruction.

Finally, establishing a winning culture must be accompanied with desired results. The standards and expectations will assist in getting the desired results, but they don't guarantee them. You can have all the standards, expectations, communication, and reinforcement you want, but if the desired results are not present then maintaining a winning culture is not possible. Remember, no matter what leadership role you are in, getting results through your people is the primary responsibility.

Establishing a winning culture should not only provide benefit to you and the organization. A winning culture should provide benefit to your team, the people that matter most. So what is the benefit? Higher compensation, benefits, and increased paid time off are probably the first to come to mind. These things are the reasons most of us go to work everyday and most companies provide these things in varying degrees. These items are critically important, but because most companies already offer these I believe that most people want more.

So what is more? The more is autonomy to do their job and not be micromanaged. The more is the reality, not the promise, of being challenged and utilized. The more is to be publicly praised and recognized as a valued contributor. The more is seeing room at the top for advancement opportunities. The more is being counted on to take on additional responsibilities, but not being overwhelmed with unreasonable demands. The more is being notified of changes within the organization that could potentially impact them. Ironically, these items relate to why top performers leave organizations according to

Marshall Loeb of MarketWatch. As a leader, it is our responsibility to utilize this potentially negative information to lead in a way consistent with creating a positive impact and higher employee retention and satisfaction.

FOCUS ON RESULTS, NOT EFFORT

This concept is one of the toughest for young leaders and young team members to grasp and buy in to. I still remember the first time I heard it, which was in the summer of 2004, and recall my general discontent and disagreement with the statement. Don't get me wrong, I still believe to this day that exceptional effort will usually lead to positive results. However, don't confuse work hours with effort. Work hours have nothing, or at least very little, to do with effort.

As a young professional, I could almost immediately delineate between the have's and the have not's. I would chuckle to myself at anyone who would promote their hours worked to their peers or superiors. A person like this is generally one that works for the longest time period during the day, but logs the least "work" hours. According to a survey by America Online and Salary.com, the average worker admits to frittering away 2.09 hours per 8-hour workday, not including lunch and scheduled break time. Salary.com calculated that employers spend $759 billion per year on salaries for which real work was expected, but not actually performed.[5] So assuming two 15-minute breaks and a one hour lunch during an eight hour workday, plus roughly two hours of lost productivity, that would require eleven and a half hours during a single day for an employer to get eight hours of productivity for which they are paying. If a worker, for example, started at 8:00 in the morning they would leave the office at 7:30 in the evening, for which most people would not be amenable. This is a reality in today's environment and something for which we have all been guilty. Whether it's talking about last night's game or an upcoming vacation, it is guilty pleasure that we all relish.

If work hours does not necessarily equate to effort, then how do we gauge effort? In most settings, effort at the individual level is extremely difficult to gauge because of the amount of people that leader has reporting to them. Of course, the leader can observe the individual's task management and activity, but ultimately this is usually a very subjective viewpoint. Sometimes experienced leaders 'just know' if their people are putting forth the necessary effort to produce positive results. This is true and is normally confirmed during water cooler discussions amongst other team members. Even if it is widely known and agreed upon, it is still a subjective gauge.

That being said, I propose that neither work hours nor effort are critically important in gauging the value of a team member. Any good leader will focus first on results. Results, whether we like or not, are what makes the world, and in particular the business world, go around. If the desired results are present, then effort is inconsequential. If results are not present, then an effective leader will then attempt to gauge the effort and make the necessary changes.

Let me try to put this in simpler terms. Take a CEO of a publicly traded company. Technically, that CEO reports to the board of directors. Indirectly, however, that CEO reports to Wall Street and the shareholders. Any MBA program will teach you that the top priority for any publicly traded company, and therefore the CEO, is to provide a return to its shareholders. So let's assume you are a shareholder that has no direct connection to the company, other than your purchase of their stock. Are you more interested in your return on investment (the results) or the effort of the CEO?

Let me put it another way. If you are on a flight during inclement weather or when the plane has a malfunction, are you more interested in the pilot landing the plane or trying really hard to land it? The answers to these questions are pretty obvious. You want a return on your stock purchase and you want the plane landed.

Effort, once again, is inconsequential so long as the desired result(s) occur. Effort is only consequential when desired results are not present. Effective leaders, therefore, focus more on results than effort.

DON'T ACCEPT MEDIOCRITY OR BELOW

This simple phrase was introduced to me by Scott Isaacs, my great friend and excellent leader from earlier in the book. The phrase is so simple, yet so insightful and detailed. Merriam-Webster defines mediocre as "of moderate or low quality, value, ability, or performance." You may be asking yourself why something so simple and obvious is included in the book. The answer is as simple as the phrase itself. It's because so many leaders don't do it. Why? Personal feelings, lack of experience or knowledge, lack of accountability or caring, or fear of confrontation are the most common reasons.

We have already defined mediocrity, at least from a dictionary. So we have essentially created a baseline. However, more insight is required. As a result, you now have three tasks related to this section. First, define what mediocrity is in your organization, business unit, or direct influence. Whether in sales, marketing, accounting, product development, human resources, etc., there has to measurement of success and failure and mediocrity is somewhere in the middle. You just have to find it. Second, identify and write down the people under your umbrella that are at or below this line and why. Last, and probably most important, once you have identified those that are mediocre or below, ask and answer the question 'what am I doing to develop them or delete them?' You absolutely must have an answer to at least one of these. If not, you are not being an effective leader. Obviously, the most preferred route for most, if not all parties involved, is to develop them. That's great. Do it. Do it now.

If it's decided that this is not the route, then you must act equally as swiftly and diligently as you would have if development had been the best option. It's unfair to your team, the organization, and most importantly, the employee to let them stay one minute longer than absolutely necessary as a 'marked' employee. You may disagree with my assessment that it's unfair to the employee, but I believe you have a duty to allow them to start the next chapter of their life and career as quickly as possible. Most people do not want to be somewhere they are not wanted, so do right by your employee. Isn't that the essence of effective leadership?

You may be asking about demotion as a compromise. Demotion is a good option only when that person was put in the position without a plan to succeed. If they were put in too early or as a reactive or interim solution, then demotion is warranted. Otherwise, my experience is that demoting individuals only prolongs the inevitable and creates a bottleneck within your team or organization. Not to mention the negative sentiment and potential internal cancer it may cause. Using phrasing from a later chapter (see page 54), demotion is definitely the exception.

You may also be asking if you can lay plans to develop and delete simultaneously. This is a high wire act where success or failure are the only outcomes. While it is probably correct to suggest that an effective leader would prepare for the best and have a backup plan for the worst, it's unadvisable to go down this road. When you're sitting on the fence, there's too much that can go wrong. For example, you create and implement a development plan for an employee and shortly thereafter the employee finds out, through whatever source, that there is also a plan to delete them. Obviously, this would hurt the employees ability to effectively do their job (which you are paying them to do), but more importantly the employees' disgruntlement could lead that employee to spread this situation or start rumors throughout the team, the division, or the organization. This is not the type of thing for which effective leaders want to put themselves in the middle. It is easier and more effective to commit to an outcome and work diligently toward that outcome for the sake and benefit of everyone involved.

CHAPTER 5

Align Responsibility, Accountability, and Authority

- ➢ **SPEAK SOFTLY AND CARRY A BIG STICK**

- ➢ **DON'T MICROMANAGE, MANAGE RESULTS THROUGH YOUR PEOPLE**

- ➢ **INTRODUCE THE *TION* BROTHERS, IF NECESSARY**

"Responsibility is the price of greatness." --- Winston Churchill

SPEAK SOFTLY AND CARRY A BIG STICK

Wow, did this one take me a long time to learn. Truth be told, I am still learning it every day. By in large, companies and leaders of these companies are generally not interested in the thoughts of middle management or below on how the company can and should improve. In many cases, senior leadership reports to The Street and members of the board and developing a plan to keep those two entities happy is likely of greatest importance. Remember, the top priority of a public company is to provide a return to its shareholders.

Unless you are one of the few that drives the vision and plans of the company, you are paid for your execution not your thoughts. However, you will not find this decree in the employee handbook. This is not to suggest that ideas are not welcome at many companies, but rather to suggest that knowing your role and responsibilities within the organization are critical to your long term success and viability.

This is where the speak softly portion comes in. As a leader in the organization, but not a senior leader, you must be very targeted in your approach to running ideas up the flagpole. It is your responsibility as a leader to coach your team of this targeted approach as well. To simplify, pick your battles and pick them carefully. The last thing most organizations want is a renegade that is operating their own agenda.

So what is a targeted approach? A targeted approach involves knowing your target audience and the potential risk versus reward of the outcome. For example, your company develops a new operating procedure for calling on clients or customers that has taken months or even years to create and test market. You and your team have been doing it your way successfully for some time. You believe this new way hinders your ability to creatively service the clients or customers because it is rigid. It requires you to deliver the company's message using its verbiage instead of delivering a personalized message from you.

You and your team eventually become frustrated with the new operating procedure and are ready to tell somebody about it. Wait. Who are you going to tell? How are you going to tell them? Were they potentially involved in the creation and deployment of the new procedure? The answer to these questions is a targeted approach. You have to anticipate the reaction before speaking and weigh the potential rewards and risks. Is the operating procedure going to change or go away as a result of you saying something? Nine times out of ten the answer is no. So, if your audience is going to potentially view your discontentment with the new operating procedure negatively, then a red flag should go up in your mind prior to engaging in the conversation. Remember, reward versus risk. If the risk to you is greater than the potential benefit to you, then proceed with extreme caution. That is if you proceed at all.

There is one way I have found, without being a senior leader, to have your thoughts and ideas heard. I have been fortunate to have this distinction on several occasions. It's carrying a big stick. No, it is not literally carrying around a big stick and threatening someone until they listen. Carrying a big stick is earned and it is earned only one way: delivering consistent, continuous results well above expectations. Organizations are not interested in losing their best performers. Organizations are interested in results. And if you and your team are delivering exceptional results then you and they are more apt to get the ear of others within the organization, including senior leaders, when you want your voice to be heard.

I have seen this time and time again and if you don't believe me, look at the top performers within your current organization or familiar organizations around you. Or recall a recent time when a top performing athlete persuaded management to make a coaching change. Kobe Bryant has done it in Los Angeles. Shaq did it in Miami. John Elway essentially did it in Denver. Why? Proven top performers get the ear of the organization, because the organization is not interested in losing its top performers.

This is not to suggest that if you have this distinction that you should abuse it. Just ask Terrell Owens, previously of the Dallas Cowboys. His time in Dallas as well as in Philadelphia with the Eagles was brief mostly due to his continual and extreme use of the stick. The organization will only tolerate its top performers to a point, the point where all marketing 101 and macro economics students come to know as the point of diminishing return.

Finally, as a leader you must intuitively know that if you've earned a stick then it is highly probable that others in your organization have earned sticks too. Don't use your stick to beat the others that carry them as well because you may quickly realize that their stick is bigger. Again, ask Terrell Owens.

DON'T MICROMANAGE, MANAGE RESULTS THROUGH YOUR PEOPLE

This is probably the most clichéd word used in the business world and certainly one of the most used words during exit interviews. Let me say this up front; micromanagers will not succeed over the long term. Period. So while subordinates are often quick to use micromanagement as a crutch or excuse for unhappiness or poor productivity, there is most definitely truth to the concept and dislike of micromanagement.

There may be certain instances in which you need to micromanage an underperformer or a critical task over the short term. Be advised, however, that you as a leader are culpable when results suffer if you choose to micromanage over the long term. Let me say that again. You as a leader are culpable when results suffer if you choose to micromanage over the long term.

First, there is a lot of denial on behalf of micromanagers about their title of being micromanagers. Second, it's hard for anybody, especially micromanagers, to accept culpability for most things. How is it then that a micromanager is culpable for lackluster results? It is the responsibility of the leader to have the right team on the bus and in the right seats. If you hired a person that requires micromanaging, then you hired the wrong person. If you inherited a person that requires micromanaging, then you have either not *casted your leadership shadow* or have not been quick enough to introduce them to the *tion brothers*. As you can plainly see, the culpability over the long term always lies with the leader.

So if micromanagers always fail over the long term, then how does a micromanager even end up in a position of leadership? It is usually a matter of timing and circumstance. Often times the leadership team is not aware of the micromanaging tendencies of the individual they bring on to lead a team or group or they plan to leave that person in place only long enough to turnaround the productivity, for which micromanagement is sometimes useful, and reassign them before long term damage is done. Other times it is a matter of being in the right place at the right time. The brass of an organization are notorious for making assumptions, especially if the geographical locations are different, about what they see on paper in the form of results without truly understanding the dynamics of a team or group. It may be that market conditions are responsible for positive results yet the leader or members of that team are rewarded on the results alone, and not the leadership behaviors that will ultimately lead to long term success.

Let me give you an example. During the housing boom between 2002 and 2006, realtors around the nation, especially in booming cities like Phoenix and Las Vegas, benefitted tremendously in commissions from home sales. Several realtors were recognized from the highest of levels of their organizations and were awarded membership into exclusive sales achievement clubs. Some obviously benefitted more than others, but the reality is that market conditions, not the realtor's abilities, were the primary reason for their success and recognition. This is a perfect example of benefitting from timing and circumstance. While the housing boom was obviously well known by most, this is not always the case within an organization. Often the short term results, not the individual's long term abilities, are promoted to the next level and thus the reason micromanagers continue to exist within organizations.

The idea of managing results through people is as simple as being the antithesis of a micromanager. If you *get the right people on the bus and in the right seats* and *cast your leadership shadow* then you will find yourself not doing the jobs of your team, but rather reaping the benefits of their productivity. This is effective leadership.

I remember early on in my managerial career a colleague of mine told me that his job as a leader was not to manage tasks, but to manage people. This has stuck with me ever since and is part of my foundation as a leader. Several years later I was leading a group of sales managers who were managing retail stores, including the store managers, selling wireless products and services. We had several store managers and even one sales manager that we termed 'super reps', because they were more interested in trying to do the jobs of their subordinates instead of doing their own job of being a sales leader. None of these "super reps", which we did not identify during the interview process, succeeded long term within our organization. They will likely not succeed long term with any other organization unless they are willing to change their ways and manage people, not tasks. It is critical to effective leadership that you manage results through your people by focusing less on being a taskmaster and more on being an effective leader.

INTRODUCE THE *TION* BROTHERS, IF NECESSARY

A revered leader in his organization, and often my go to person for business and leadership discussions and advice, Scott Isaacs, often jokes about introducing his people to the *tion* brothers (pronounced Shawn). At first, I too thought it was a joke. The reality is that it's not and sometimes it's a key component of effective leadership.

Ineffective leaders often do themselves, the team, and the person or people in question a disservice by not addressing unproductive or cancerous team members, thus making the entire team and your leadership efforts less effective. Effective leaders will see a challenge with a team member or group of team members, address them quickly, make changes quickly, if necessary, and keep the focus and direction of the team in line with the vision of that leader. The concept of the *tion* brothers is simple. Those of you with human resource knowledge, especially in larger organizations, might call it progressive discipline. The first *tion* brother is explana*tion*. It is critical to effective leadership that an unproductive and/or cancerous team member quickly be given an explanation of their deficiency and be given the opportunity to quickly correct the behavior. Note the consistent use of the word quickly. An effective leader will sniff these things out, address them on the spot, and expect an immediate turnaround.

The second *tion* brother is documenta*tion*. Documentation has to be an afterthought this day in age. In this case, meaning an absolute requirement. Besides its necessity in today's environment, it maintains a tactical purpose. All of us have been children and many of us have children of our own. Think about the levels of discipline that either you endured as a child or that you use with your children. For example, your child needs to clean their room. You politely ask your child to clean their room and then you walk away. You check back 10 minutes later and your child has promptly done nothing. This time you raise your voice a little, again ask the child to clean their room, and again walk away. You check back five minutes later and once again your child has done nothing. You are now becoming increasingly frustrated and this time you threaten to take away the child's favorite toy or video game or threaten to spank them, depending on your methodology and beliefs. You again check back in five minutes and your child has made significant progress in cleaning their room. Now, it's likely that you are not going to document your child's behavior and put it in the personnel file. The point is that seeking the least obtrusive discipline to correct the behavior and documenting those levels along the way is critical to the organization and also to the individual's understanding, acceptance, and ability and willingness to correct the behavior(s).

The final *tion* brother is termina*tion*. If you are a leader or desire to be one, which I assume based on the fact that you made it this far in the guide, then this is one of the toughest things you will have to do. Generally speaking, you are affecting someone's livelihood and ability to provide the basic necessities to oneself and one's family. This may seem a little over dramatic, but ask someone who has been terminated before. Notice that I said you as a leader are "affecting". It's an important distinction because you are not 'causing' or 'prohibiting', you are simply 'affecting', which is to suggest that you are part of the process. I have often heard that a manager or leader does not fire anyone, but rather the individual fires themselves. The premise here is that the individual's productivity and/or attitude declines to the point where they 'fire themselves'. Theoretically, this may be true. However, the reality is that you as a leader or manager have to face this person eye-to-eye and announce to them that they are no longer part of the team, group, or organization.

If leadership were easy, then everyone would do it. As a leader, it's a normal human emotion to feel guilty or try to justify a termination in an attempt to deflect or reassign the negative emotions. Based on my experience, this is one part of leadership that never gets easier. However, effective leadership absolutely demands it.

An effective leader understands the theory of utilitarianism, popularized by British philosopher John Stuart Mill, which states "actions are right to the degree that they tend to promote the greatest good for the greatest number."[6] In other words, an effective leader takes action to promote what they believe is best for the team or group, not an individual, and often times this requires acting to remove an individual or multiple individuals for the good of the team or group.

Having stated all of this, it is important for an effective leader to make sure that the unproductive or cancerous (maybe counterproductive) behaviors are in fact behaviors and not training or coaching deficiencies. This is done during the explanation process at which time you will solicit feedback. Consider the discussion about levels of discipline with children. In the previous example, it was assumed that the child was of an age where they were capable of not only understanding the directions, but also of executing on the task.

For this discussion, let's assume the child is one year old. A one year old is generally not capable of accepting directions to clean their room and is even more likely not to understand the tasks required to clean their room. So in this case the child probably does not have counterproductive behaviors, but rather requires teaching and coaching by the parent to get them to understand both the direction to clean their room and the tasks required to clean it. The same applies for adults in a work setting. As much as an individual deserves to quickly be removed for counterproductive behaviors, they deserve to immediately receive the training and coaching necessary to respond to direction and complete tasks to effectively perform their job duties.

CHAPTER 6

Disciplined Time and Energy

- ➢ USE, BUT DON'T OVERUSE TODAY'S TECHNOLOGY TO COMMUNICATE

- ➢ USE THE RULE WHEN MAKING DECISIONS, BUT DON'T FORGET THE EXCEPTION

- ➢ ADAPT AND OVERCOME

"The time to repair the roof is when the sun is shining." --- *JFK*

USE, BUT DON'T OVERUSE TODAY'S TECHNOLOGY TO COMMUNICATE

Email, text messaging, and conference calls are excellent technological resources especially for communicating with the masses. Email specifically is useful not only for mass communications, but also for documentation purposes. Text messaging is a quick way to communicate short messages to individuals or groups. The most recent estimates by CTIA-The Wireless Association indicate that 28.8 billion text messages are sent per month, which is nearly 241 billion per year. Both of these extremely effective non-verbal communication methods and definitely have their usefulness.

Conversely, conference calls are generally an effective verbal communication tool. Conference calls are beneficial because they easily service small groups or group sizes into the thousands that are not in close proximity to one another. Each of these technological resources has the flexibility to be used intercontinentally, which is especially pleasing given the tremendous growth in globalization.

The fact of the matter is that I use all three of the resources everyday. Sometimes I use them by choice and sometimes others initiate the communication. I do not deny their usefulness, effectiveness, and flexibility. However, my message is not one of denial, but rather of caution.

A primary characteristic, and often times *the* primary characteristic, of quality leadership is effective communication with team members. As a rule, the most effective communication method is face-to-face interaction. I see too many leaders in today's world hiding behind email or conference calls and not physically participating in the mentoring and growth of their team members. Obviously the increased popularity of virtual offices has hindered this ability, but face-to-face interactions and one-on-one telephone conversations are still the most effective and desirable communication methods of quality leaders.

In the context of all of this, do not lose sight of the lost productivity that comes as a result of excessive emails, text messages, and conference calls. In past work environments it was not unusual for me to receive 50 to 100 emails per day. Many of you may receive far greater numbers than that. My job was mostly out of the office and in the field so 50 to 100 emails per day stacked up pretty quickly. It was usually a one to two hour task daily to muddle through the emails and decipher which information was important and actionable and which could immediately receive the delete button treatment.

Conference calls are another staple in corporate life that I have known to be well overused. I once worked for a company in the wireless industry that had all its managers participate in a conference call every morning, excluding Sunday. The idea behind the calls was that the owner's would have their call first, then the regional directors would have a call with their sales managers, then the sales managers would have a call with their store managers. This way, each manager in the company would know the content of the previous calls and all managers would be on the same page for the day.

The first call would start at 9:00am and participation included me, the three owners, and the other regional director. At 9:45am, my regional director peer and I would have a call with our sales managers. At 10:30am the sales managers would have a call with their store managers. Keep in mind that most stores opened at 9:00am, so managers were taking the calls during operating hours. The owners and store managers were only on one call per day, but the directors and sales managers were on two calls per day. The prep time each morning to be prepared for the discussions amounted to a minimum of 30 minutes. So the directors and sales managers would spend a minimum of 12 hours per week either prepping for the call or participating in a call itself. Store managers would spend nearly the equivalent of a full work day (eight hours) performing the same duties. All of this was in addition to a daily phone call we would receive from our superiors who were 'just checking in'.

There were three basic topics that led to the content of each call. First, there would be a discussion of the previous day's sales and the successes or failures that led to those sales. The second topic would be on what we were going to do to either replicate the successes or fix the failures of the previous day's sales. Lastly, we would discuss any operational focuses that needed to be planned and/or executed. The thoughts and intentions behind the calls were solid, but the lost productivity each day for the majority of our personnel severely diminished our ability to reach our goals.

The combination of emails and conference calls consumed between 25 and 40 percent of our normal workday. I can speak from experience and tell you that this was a colossal waste of time and morale deflator. This would force us to work additional hours to produce the results we needed or would decrease our effectiveness if we didn't work the additional hours. These calls also had a secondary effect. Morale decreased not only because we had to participate six days a week, including days off, but because these calls often had a negative tone due to poor sales from the previous day.

Even though I vehemently disagreed with the daily call concept for the aforementioned reasons, I did appreciate the owners' conviction that this was a positive step in moving the company forward. After all, it was their money and in a privately held company the owner's have the right to set the company direction in any fashion they choose within the boundaries of the law.

We discussed earlier in the guide that an effective leader does not micromanage, but rather hires efficient and effective personnel, trains and coaches them well, holds them accountable and allows them to essentially produce the results or not. Daily conference calls, or excessive conference calls, are classic examples of micromanagement and stray far way from many of the concepts discussed in this guide.

USE THE RULE WHEN MAKING DECISIONS, BUT DON'T FORGET THE EXCEPTION

Statistics suggest that most men make decisions based more on fact (or logic) and most women make decisions based more on emotion. This argument is clearly a topic for another book. The point I want to make here is not about gender, but rather that most decisions are made with either fact-based or emotion-based criteria.

The 'rule' when making decisions in a business environment is to make them based on facts. Why? The list is close to never ending but primarily because it shows fairness and respect to your superiors, peers, and, most importantly, your subordinates. Secondarily, it keeps you in good graces with the HR department and allows for a consistent, thoughtful approach to decision making.

If all of these benefits exist to making decisions based on facts, then why aren't all decisions made on facts alone? The simple answer is that we are all human beings and the impropriety of emotions is nearly impossible to avoid. The more complicated answer, although not that complicated, is that facts don't take into consideration hindsight, potential, character, intent, experience, or longevity. In short, facts eliminate human experience and emotion, which can serve both as positive or negative depending on the circumstance. Fact-based decision making, "the rule", is a must for all successful leaders.

Emotion-based decisions, the 'exception', are also required to be an effective leader. At the very least, combine emotion with facts.

As we identified in the last paragraph, facts eliminate human experience and emotion. Emotion-based decisions clearly include these. Let me use an example from one of my past leadership roles to help clarify an emotion-based decision. Bobby Hollis was a former subordinate of mine at Alltel Wireless. He had been with the company for about three years when he applied for and earned a position on my team. He was a developing employee with no past problems with the company. About one year into his tenure on my team, I receive a call from the corporate security team detailing company policies that Bobby had recently broken that were most certainly terminable offenses.

A couple of weeks later Bobby was interrogated for about an hour, with me present, by the corporate security team. I had never witnessed an employee of a public company be treated so poorly. I could better understand if he had breached national security or had been a witness to or an accomplice of a crime. But this was an $11 billion company where no more than $150 was involved. At the end of the interrogation it was clear that Bobby had in fact broken company policy on two different occasions, one involving crediting a customer's account inconsistent with company policy and the other was for purchasing discounted accessories.

I walked away from the meeting knowing the facts, for which I was disappointed with Bobby. I also walked away from the meeting disgusted with the way my employee was treated by the interrogator. Having worked with Bobby first hand for the past year, I knew the kind of decent person he was. Company policy, precedence, and the HR department all pointed toward immediate termination. On facts alone, this was clearly the correct decision. However, I allowed emotion to become involved and, in my opinion, justifiably so. Bobby was a young man that should have known better, but also had a youthful ignorance about him that suggested to me that his acts were not done maliciously. He was and is a man of character that made some poor choices.

I liked Bobby and knew that he would be a future leader in the organization if given the opportunity to stay. I immediately went to my boss and the HR department and fought for Bobby's employment. I was not only fighting for him, I was putting my integrity and career on the line by doing so. After numerous calls and meetings, the HR department and I negotiated to let Bobby stay under the condition that he be given a final written warning and required to attend additional training on company policies and behavioral expectations. Bobby remains with Alltel Wireless today and has grown into a leader with an impeccable record since this incident.

Should I have terminated Bobby? Should the organization have stood firmer and required me to terminate him? Should the organization take any of the blame? Should I take any of the blame? Did I put my employees' well-being ahead of the company's? Did I put my own well-being ahead of the company's? Did I let emotion get the best of me?

I am not sure there is a correct answer to any of these questions. However, at that particular point in time and under the given circumstances I strongly believe I made the right decision. I believe to this day that I made the right decision. The facts suggested termination. The emotions suggested otherwise. This is not your excuse to use subjectivity in every decision, but it is your excuse to be a human being and a leader. After all, the main thing that separates us as human beings from all other forms of life is that we have the ability to reason.

ADAPT AND OVERCOME

A good friend of mine and highly successful former head baseball coach at Midland College in Texas and Trinidad State Junior College in Colorado, Steve Ramharter, used this phrase as an unofficial mantra of his baseball programs. It was partially interpreted from the U.S. Marines unofficial mantra of improvise, adapt and overcome, which was derived well in the past because Marines generally received Army hand-me-downs and were poorly equipped.[7] It has been years since I was involved with the Midland College baseball program, but that mantra resonated with me profoundly. To me, it meant that not all situations, if any, are going to be perfect and therefore one must adapt to the imperfection and overcome it to achieve desired results.

Adapt and overcome has been a continued area of opportunity for many in leadership, including myself. Why? Inherently, we all believe that we are right and know what needs to be done in most situations. So when we get someone, namely a superior, who tells us to do something a different way than we 'know is right', we generally become skeptical, frustrated, and dismissive.

In a previous work life, I worked for a company in which I probably disagreed more than I agreed with our operating procedures and practices. Recall the conference calls we had six days a week with our senior leadership followed up by a conference call with our direct reports. The purpose of these calls, as it was explained to me, was to discuss and share the successes and opportunities of the previous days' sales and to discuss any outstanding operations focuses.

Theoretically, the concept was not that bad. Practically, it was a nightmare. Often times it would become a forum for negativity and ultimately served more as a morale demoralizer than a morale booster. It was micromanagement, plain and simple.

As we know from our previous discussion on why people leave, micromanagement is a top reason why people decide to go elsewhere. Plus, it took everyone away from the core business needs. In my opinion, it was a bad decision to start these calls and a worse decision to continue them. While these calls represented poor leadership choices, not necessarily poor leaders, it was equally as poor of a leadership choice for me not to adapt and overcome to these daily conference calls.

The bottom line is that in any environment you are often going to be disappointed with the decisions that are made above you. This is true from day one and continues throughout our lives. It is not just exclusive to the business world. The most effective leaders adapt to and overcome questionable decisions by seeking to understand the reason for and impact of the decision. They also try to find the positive, or at least mitigate the negative, of the decision.

CHAPTER 7

Motivation and Inspiration

➢ **DO THE LITTLE THINGS**

➢ **SPEAK THEIR LANGUAGE**

➢ **SHOW YOUR PERSONAL SIDE**

➢ **HAVE PASSION**

"They may forget what you said, but they will never forget how you made them feel." --- Carl W. Buechner

DO THE LITTLE THINGS

During the depression years of the late 1920's and continuing through most of the 1930's, the goal of working men was to simply provide the basics of life to their families. Food, clothing, and respectable living conditions were the order of the day. Today's world is a far cry from the depression era and while the basic staples of life still remain, it's vacation time, rewards and recognition, stable work environments, company cars, 401k's, and sick time and paid time off (PTO) that rule the day. No question that entitlement is prevalent in today's world.

Numerous books and articles have been written as to why this dynamic has progressed as it has. It started with the post-war baby boomer generation (born between 1946 and 1964), escalated with generation X (born between 1965 and 1981), and has reached an all-time high with the millennial's (born in the 80's and early 90's). It is not necessarily important for our purposes to discuss why this dynamic exists, but rather to focus on knowing that it exists and understanding that leadership roles are more different today than in any other time in our history. This does not come as good news for leaders still in the workforce that were born before World War II and even to many of the early boomers.

Today's environment requires leaders to not just be stewards of the company's needs and wants, it requires them to be advocates of the personal desires of team members. It used to be good enough to have a job and get paid for doing it, which was a big thing. To be advocates of the personal desires of team members you must *do the little things.* For example, periodically tracking your subordinate's vacation time and getting a commitment from them to take it.

Many leaders, including several for whom I have worked, would never consider going to their subordinates and strongly encouraging or even requiring them to take their vacation time. The thought process is that if they require them to use their vacation time then that is less productivity that they are going to get out of that individual. Another thought process is that an employee is paid to work and not to take vacation. While these two things may be true, it is simply ignorant thinking for successful leaders. Gen X'ers and millenial's covet their vacation time and consider it a right, not a privilege. So why fight it? You can score points as a leader by encouraging them and gaining commitment from them to take that vacation time. Not only does it score you points, it's a statistical fact that employees that take vacation and unplug periodically throughout the year are more productive when they are working.

Small rewards such as game, movie or theatre tickets, a restaurant or shopping gift card, an award, certificate or trophy presented in front of team members, paid time off, birthday, anniversary and holiday well wishes, and gifts are all little things you can do as a leader to make team members more positive not only about you, but also about their work environment. A positive work environment generally leads to greater productivity.

Genuinely promoting a work/life balance is another example doing a little thing. This can include encouraging team members to take their vacation, but encompasses so many other facets. Remember, eating, providing clothing, and living in respectable conditions are no longer good enough. People no longer live to work, they work to live. An effective leader, no matter how much they may dislike this new culture, will adjust and be an advocate of the personal desires of their team. Allowing team members to display pictures of their family in their work area, seeking information about a team members' family life, inviting family members to company events, and allowing time off for birthdays, anniversaries, and children's events are examples, although not all-inclusive, of promoting a work/life balance as a leader.

I provided examples of doing the little things to provoke thought about other ways you as a leader can successfully perform this task. It is important for the leader to be genuine in doing the little things, but also should not feel guilty about the return efforts and results that you are seeking as a result of doing those little things. In the space below, I encourage you to write a list of "little things" that both fit into your style or into your current situation AND that you are willing to perform.

_____

_____

_____

_____

_____

_____

_____

_____

Of all the ideas detailed in this guide, doing the little things has probably earned me more loyalty and more respect than any other one thing. If I had a job opening today, there are individuals that have previously been on my team that I could call that would almost certainly leave their current post to join my team. This is not arrogance. It is a level of leadership in which treating people with fairness and respect, combined with coaching them to results and desired compensation, will almost always yield loyalty well beyond what you as the leader contributed in the first place.

Put another way, if I turned you on to an investment in which you could invest $1,000 up front and two years later you would start receiving $100 per month for the next 10 years, would you invest? This is $1,200 per year over a 10-year span on an initial investment of only $1,000. Assuming you had performed your due diligence and had found little to no flaws, of course you would take this investment. While it's more difficult to put mathematical outcome on people compared to an investment, being an effective leader and doing the little things will give you a return on investment over the long-term far greater than your initial investment.

As the French philosopher Simone De Beauvoir once said, "don't gamble on the future, act now, without delay." So go out today and start laying the foundation for your return on investment by *doing the little things*.

SPEAK THEIR LANGUAGE

One might assume that I am mean foreign languages such as Spanish, French, or Japanese. These, as well other languages, can be an extremely beneficial in the workplace and depending on your job title and industry may even be a requirement or strong suggestion. Without underestimating the importance of speaking a foreign language or two, the language I speak of is the language of your workforce. Specifically, the newest generation hitting the workforce coded simply as mellinial's.

No leadership book written after the turn of the 21st century can be complete without addressing this unique, mysterious group. Tom Brokaw of NBC News appropriately labeled the American men who fought in World War II as the "Greatest Generation". Of course this could be argued on many levels. We have seen many generations in our over three century history contribute heftily to the growth and vitality of the United States of America. Although time will tell, at the time of publication I don't believe anyone, except maybe those inside this generation, would even give a vote to the millennial generation.

This generation is comprised of individuals born in the 80's and early 90's. CBS News' Morley Safer aired a segment on 60 Minutes dedicated solely to this group. I recommend pulling the transcripts from the Web or viewing it on You Tube. A fair assumption is that if you are reading this book you have the intellect to know that not every person born during this time period encompasses all the characteristics of a millennial, good or bad.

On a positive note, millennial's are important to today's workforce because of their tech savviness and ability to adapt to change. However, with the good comes the bad. After reading or viewing Shafer's piece, you will likely inherit the general distain for this group within the workplace. As a leader, you may already be living it on a daily basis. I know I have. You may even be within this group, and if so, we forgive you. The perceived negative characteristics of this group include entitlement, desire for excessive praise, consistent tardiness and/or truancy, and an uncanny habit of jumping ship out of an organization if something doesn't go their way. The reasons for these traits are numerous and generally go way beyond my skill level and expertise.

As an editorial aside, I do subscribe to the theory that keeping score, encouraging winning, learning from losing, not having every kid play once they reach a certain level, and not giving participatory trophies are healthy for most children and society in general. Call me old fashion.

SHOW YOUR PERSONAL SIDE

This is one of the most controversial topics of leadership that I have come across in my years in the business and academic worlds. Many that oppose my view would say that work is work and home is home. There is, of course, some truth to this. We have a job to do at work and we have a job to do at home.

One of my arguments to this opposition is that you frequently discuss the people and happenings at work with your spouse and family, so why isn't okay to discuss the people and happenings at home with your colleagues and team members at work? The answer is that it is okay. It's okay, and even encouraged, to have pictures of your family on your desk. It's okay to share information about weekend trips or vacations. It's okay to speak about the loss of a family member or pet. It's okay to share details of your son's baseball game or your daughter's dance recital. It's okay to say you lounged around and watched TV or read a book. In other words, it's okay to be a human being. These things are what people do. This is what your team members do.

It's time that this became a real leadership trait. It allows you as the leader to have dialogue with your team members outside of the daily grind of work. It allows you to be seen as a person, similar to them. It also opens up the door, but does not require them, to share what is important to them with you. I am certainly not suggesting that work should become secondary to this sharing, rather the contrary. I am suggesting that it be part of your routine, when work or deadlines may not be imminent.

My other argument is that in today's culture people want to work for human beings. In the past, there was a clear line drawn between leader and follower, manager and employee and in some cases even between husband and wife. Even if you go to Walgreen's or TJ Maxx today, you will hear the manager paged over the loudspeaker as Mr. Smith or Mrs. Jones. These organizations clearly still have that line, which I am not necessarily saying is all bad.

However, in today's environment, especially with the approximately 60 million strong millennial's generation, it requires a softer, more what's in it for them approach from leadership. Why is this? While there are various theories and probably even more psychobabble, I believe it's largely because they were raised in a more coddled and doting environment than past generations. In fact, several of today's more prominent companies are hiring consultants to help them deal with this new brand of employee that will only accept yes for an answer and require that they come first. I am not suggesting I agree with this new leadership requirement. In fact, I have extensive experience with millennial's and for the most part I have been less than impressed, especially with the ones born in the late eighties and first half of the nineties. However, we must all accept this reality and adapt our styles if we are going to be effective leaders for years to come. (Footnote: when I say adapt be sure not to interpret that as change our entire style. There are still results to get and molding your team into your style is equally as important as adapting to them).

So how do we adapt our style without losing effectiveness? We can use praise more often than constructive coaching. We can praise in public and punish in private. We can show interest, without forcing dialogue, in their personal goals and hobbies. We can create a plan for their growth and development. There are probably thousands of things we as leaders could do. We could certainly execute on the practices in this book. One of the best, if not the best, ways to adapt your style while maintaining or even improving your effectiveness is to show your personal side early and often in your leadership roles.

HAVE PASSION

There are two reasons I chose to put this chapter on passion last. First, without it everything you have read and acquired up to this point is nearly meaningless. Second, the most common trait of effective leaders is a passion for leading people to achieve a common goal. Even if they are weak in other areas, their passion usually drives them and the team to success.

Dictionary.com defines passion as an intense, driving, or overmastering feeling or conviction. The most effective leaders have a passion. However, their passion may differ. They may have passion for their particular job, their company, their product or service, or simply winning. They may have passion not just for one of these, but several. However, the most effective leaders have passion in one or several of these areas in addition to the passion they have for leading people. Leading another human being, including raising children, is quite simply one of the most difficult things we do in our lives. As difficult, or even more difficult than leading a person, is to care more about their personal and professional growth and success than you do your own. This is my definition of leadership.

I will close by saying that passion cannot be fabricated. You can't have it some days and not others. It can't be turned on and off like a light switch. It's very hard, although not impossible, to learn passion from others. In my humble opinion, truly effective, admired, and respected leaders have a true passion only when it's inside their heart, mind, and soul, yet it's usually visible for the entire world to see. My advice: do something for which you have an innate passion.

References

[1] http://www.managementmalpractice.com/in_the_news.php

[2] http://www.microsoft.com/smallbusiness/resources/expert/strauss092205.mspx

[3] Bill Walsh: The Legacy of "The Genius", Michael Yermus, 10/23/2004

[4] http://www.canismajor.com/dog/iditarod.html

[5] Wasted Time At Work Costing Companies Billions, Dan Malachowski, Salary.com, Monday, July 11, 2005

[6] http://webs.wofford.edu/kaycd/ethics/util.htm

[7] http://www.answers.com/topic/improvise-adapt-and-overcome